What to do WHEN the PROBLEM is... YOU

What To Do When The Problem Is You?
Copyright © 2024 Janak Alford
Illustrations by Daria Yudina

This book and the accompanying illustrations are a work of fiction. Any representations or likenesses of any person, living or dead, are purely coincidental. Janak Alford asserts the moral right to be recognized as the author of this work. All rights reserved. No part of this publication may be reproduced, stored in a retrieval system, or transmitted in any form or by any means, electronic, mechanical, photocopying, recording, or otherwise, without the prior written permission of the author.

Declaration of Human Origin
This book, encompassing all textual content and imagery, is the product of human creativity and intellect. No part of this publication utilized Artificial Intelligence systems or Generative AI technologies in its creation or development.

Paperback ISBN: 978-1-7779796-4-5
Published by Symaiotics Corporation

This book is dedicated to **you**.

Please accept these words as a friendly reminder of the obstacles we each face in our quest to grow as individuals and leaders. You might recognize a part of yourself in each challenge and, I hope, in every solution offered.

It is shared with love, a dash of humor, and a commitment to our mutual growth.

Criticism

Do you belittle and shout,
blame and insult,
and see all of your issues
as everyone's fault?

Negativity

Do you focus on just a problem or two, while ignoring all the good things around you?

Unreliability

Do you see others trying
and hope they will fail,
or promise support
and suddenly bail?

Blaming

How about when things
don't go just right,
do you puff up your chest
and go pick a fight?

Apathy

Do you just go work to bring home a cheque, and go through the motions without giving a heck?

Close-Mindedness

Do you squash new ideas
which are outside your skills,
till your whole team
just runs for the hills?

Indifference

**Do you hide away from all
the new things you should know,
and avoid learning skills
that will help you to grow?**

Toxicity

When faced with difference
do you discriminate,
till your place of work
becomes one of hate?

Pessimism

―◦―

**Do you scoff and grumble
'That won't ever fly!',
and give up the plan
without even a try?**

―◦―

If any of the above
sound like they're true,
then you've probably guessed it...
The problem is *you*!

Self-Realization

―○―

**So,
what can you do?**

―○―

Proactivity

**Grab a pencil and paper
or type on your keys,
and get down to work
just as quick as you please.**

Inclusion

**Gather your team,
each with their view,
it takes all kinds
to do anything new.**

Empathy

Make a safe space where you all take turns, and listen to everyone's fears and concerns.

Enthusiasm

**Build up a big vision
with everyone there,
and make it ambitious,
as much as you dare!**

Iterative Growth

Start off quite early, quickly, and small, don't be overwhelmed by planning it all.

Transparency

Write down your big plans so that new people know, and everyone remembers when you're all feeling low.

Agility

Be willing to change your plan when it's time, make constant adjustments but don't turn on a dime.

Continual Learning

Invest in your people
to learn something new,
and never forget
that this includes you.

Collaboration

No matter your station, your rank, or your role, roll up your sleeves to achieve your big goal.

Change Management

Start to make change for goodness' sake, and map out the risks you're willing to take.

Innovation

Invest in some tools
to make it go fast,
and set a few processes
so that it will last.

Self-Motivation

Today's a new day
with nothing to lose,
and lucky for you,
you still get to choose.

Positivity

**Try to be positive
in all that you do,
and you'll see soon enough...
the solution is *you*!**

The End

About the Author

Janak Alford is an author, entrepreneur, and technologist.

By day, he helps major public sector organizations adopt a digital mindset and transform their business processes.

By vocation he is a full-stack developer, innovator, product designer, and a constant learner.

www.ingramcontent.com/pod-product-compliance
Lightning Source LLC
Chambersburg PA
CBHW080325080526
44585CB00021B/2482